GW01376905

First published in Great Britain in 1996 by
BROCKHAMPTON PRESS,
20 Bloomsbury Street,
London WC1B 3QA.
a member of the Hodder Headline Group,

This series of little gift books was made by Frances Banfield, Andrea P.A. Belloli, Polly Boyd, Kate Brown, Stefano Carantini, Laurel Clark, Penny Clarke, Clive Collins, Jack Cooper, Melanie Cumming, Nick Diggory, John Dunne, Deborah Gill, David Goodman, Paul Gregory, Douglas Hall, Lucinda Hawksley, Maureen Hill, Dennis Hovell, Dicky Howett, Nick Hutchison, Douglas Ingram, Helen Johnson, C.M. Lee, Simon London, Irene Lyford, John Maxwell, Patrick McCreeth, Morse Modaberi, Tara Neill, Sonya Newland, Anne Newman, Grant Oliver, Ian Powling, Terry Price, Michelle Rogers, Mike Seabrook, Nigel Soper, Karen Sullivan and Nick Wells.

Compilation and selection copyright © 1996 Brockhampton Press.

All rights reserved. No part of this publication may be reproduced, stored in a retrieval system, or transmitted in any form or by any means, without the prior written permission of the copyright holder.

ISBN 1 86019 429X

A copy of the CIP data is available from the British Library upon request.
Produced for Brockhampton Press by Flame Tree Publishing,
a part of The Foundry Creative Media Company Limited,
The Long House, Antrobus Road, Chiswick W4 5HY.

Printed and bound in Italy by L.E.G.O. Spa.

THE LITTLE BOOK OF
Inspiration

Selected by Karen Sullivan

BROCKHAMPTON PRESS

May the Great Mystery make sunrise in your heart.

Sioux Indian saying

What a delight it is
When, borrowing
Rare writings from a friend,
I open out
The first sheet.

Tachibana Akemi, *Poems of Solitary Delights*

When you do not know what you are doing and what you are doing is the best — that is inspiration.

Robert Bresson

Hope, the patent medicine
For disease, disaster, sin.

Wallace Rice

Hope is the feeling you have that
the feeling you have isn't permanent.

Jean Kerr, *Finishing Touches*

The natural flights of the human mind are not from pleasure to pleasure, but from hope to hope.
Samuel Johnson

Ah, Hope! What would life be, stripped of thy encouraging smiles, that teach us to look behind the dark clouds of to-day, for the golden beams that are to gild the morrow.
Susanna Moodie

Let us be grateful to people who make us happy; they are the charming gardeners who make our souls blossom.
Marcel Proust

Give a man health and a course to steer; and he'll never stop to trouble about whether he's happy or not.
George Bernard Shaw

Happiness makes up in height what it lacks in length.
Robert Frost

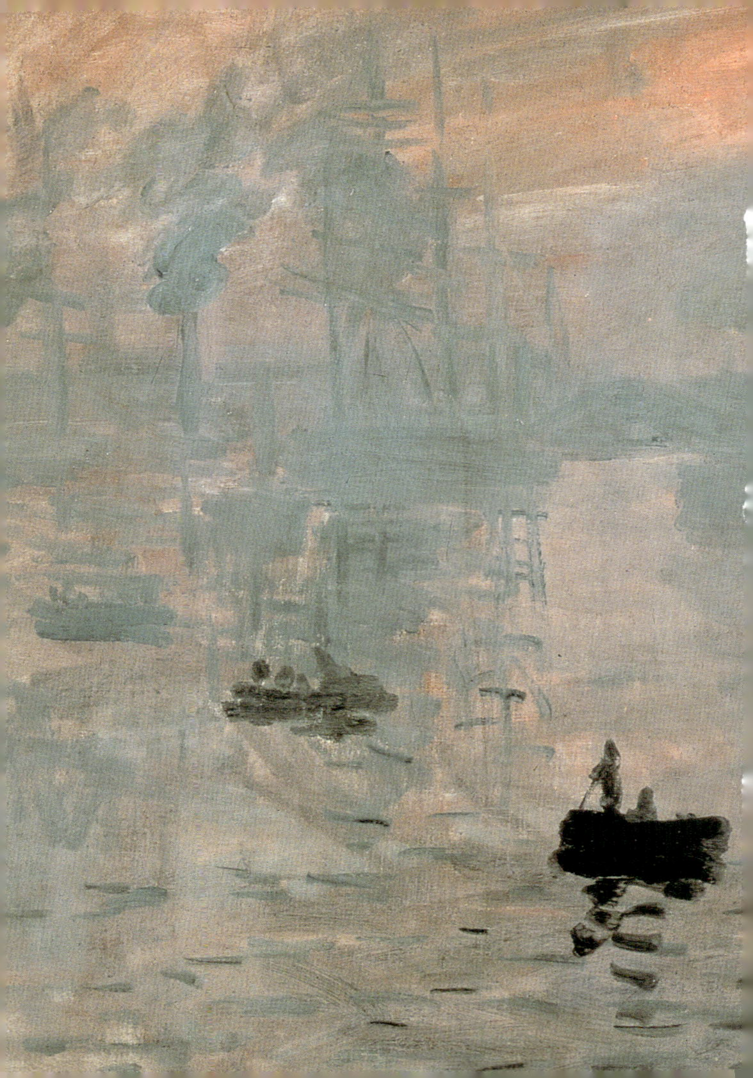

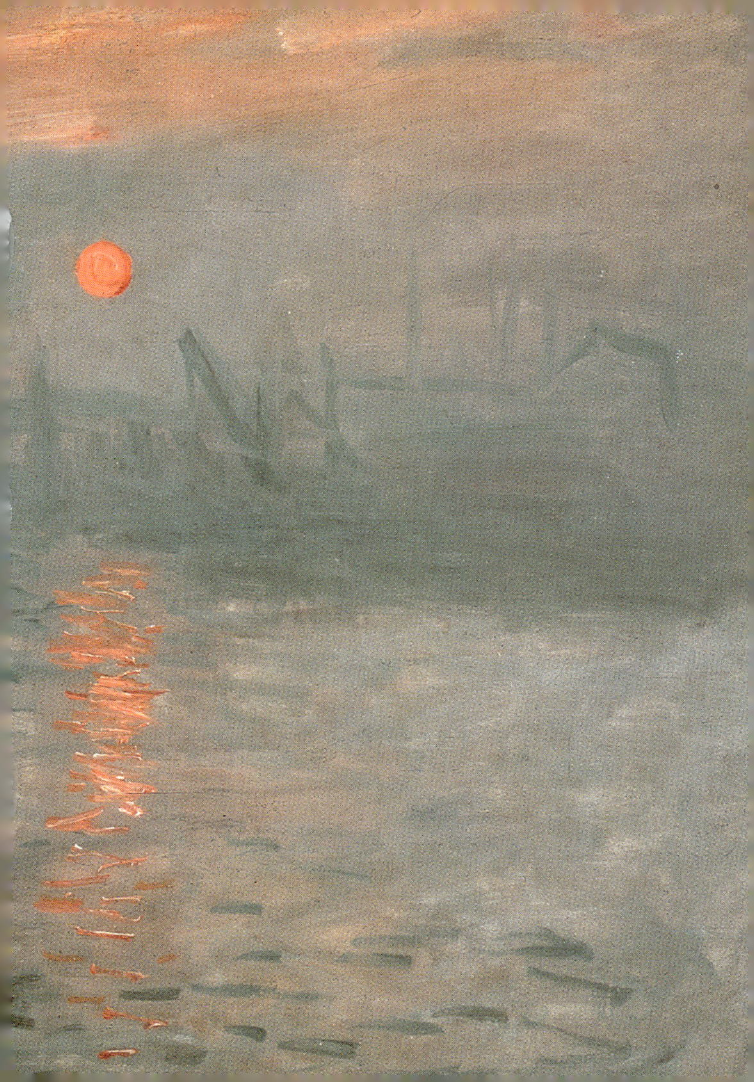

There is no limit to what a man can do so long as he
does not care a straw who gets the credit for it.

C. E. Montague

I recommend to you to take care of the minutes;
for hours will take care of themselves.

Lord Chesterfield

Take care to sell your horse before he dies.
The art of life is passing losses on.

Robert Frost

The torpid artist seeks inspiration at any cost, by virtue
or by vice, by friend or by fiend, by prayer or by wine.

Ralph Waldo Emerson

Invention flags, his brain goes muddy,
And black despair succeeds brown study.

William Congreve

Happiness was not made to be boasted, but enjoyed.
Therefore tho' others count me miserable,
I will not believe them if I know and feel myself to be
happy; nor fear them.

Thomas Traherne

Even if happiness forgets you a little bit, never
completely forget about it.

Jacques Prévert

Life can only be understood backwards:
but it must be lived forwards.
Soren Kierkegaard, *Stages on Life's Way*

Oh, the comfort, the inexpressible comfort of feeling
safe with a person, having neither to weigh thoughts
nor measure words, but pouring them all right out,
just as they are, chaff and grain together; certain that a
faithful hand will take and sift them, keep what is
worth keeping, and then with the breath of kindness
blow the rest away.
Dinah Craik

For what human ill does not dawn
seem to be an alleviation?
Thornton Wilder, *The Bridge of San Luis Rey*

Happiness is a wine of the rarest vintage,
and seems insipid to a vulgar taste.
Logan Pearsall Smith

── THE LITTLE BOOK OF INSPIRATION ──

Love is like the wild rose-briar;
Friendship like the holly-tree.
The holly is dark when the rose-briar blooms,
But which will bloom most constantly?

Emily Brontë

Accountability in friendship is the equivalent of love without strategy.

Anita Brookner

Live all you can; it's a mistake not to. It doesn't so much matter what you do in particular, so long as you have had your life. If you haven't had that, what have you had?

Henry James, *The Ambassadors*

What a delight it is
When, spreading paper,
I take my brush
And find my hand
Better than I thought.

Tachibana Akemi, *Poems of Solitary Delights*

To regret one's own experiences is to arrest one's own development. To deny one's own experiences is to put a lie into the lips of one's own life. It is no less than a denial of the soul.

Oscar Wilde, *De Profundis*

THE LITTLE BOOK OF INSPIRATION

Men go abroad to wonder at the height of mountains,
at the huge waves of the sea,
at the long courses of the rivers,
at the vast compasses of the ocean,
at the circular motion of the stars,
and they pass by themselves without wondering.

Augustine of Hippo

What is true in the lamplight is
not always true in the sunlight.

Joseph Joubert, *Pensées*

All love that has not friendship for its base,
Is like a mansion built upon the sand.

Ella Wheeler Wilcox

The spirit of wisdom cannot be delineated with pen and ink, no more than a sound can be painted, or the wind grasped in the hollow of the hand.

John Sparrow, Preface to *Boehme's Signatura Rerum*

Slender at first, they quickly gather force,
Growing in richness as they run their course;
Once started, they do not turn back again:
Rivers, and years, and friendships with good men.

Sanskrit poem

Wisdom is like electricity. There is no permanently wise man, but men capable of wisdom, who, being put into certain company, or other favorable conditions, become wise for a short time, as glasses rubbed acquire electric power for a while.

Ralph Waldo Emerson

Wear your worries like a loose garment.

Anonymous

Who know the world live alone.

Ali ibn Abu Talib

Nine-tenths of wisdom consists in being wise in time.

Theodore Roosevelt

The fear of the Lord is the beginning of wisdom.

Psalms, CXI:10.

It is the province of knowledge to speak, and it is the privilege of wisdom to listen.

Oliver Wendell Holmes Sr

Out of the closets and into the museums, libraries, architectural monuments, concert halls, bookstores, recording studios and film studios of the world. Everything belongs to the inspired and dedicated thief…Words, colours, light, sounds, stone, wood, bronze belong to the living artist. They belong to anyone who can use them. Loot the Louvre! A bas l'originalité, the sterile and assertive ego that imprisons us as it creates. Vive le sol — pure, shameless, total. We are not responsible. Steal anything in sight.

William Burroughs

People are beginning to see that the first requisite to success in life is to be a good animal.

Herbert Spencer

Wisdom we know is the knowledge of good and evil —
not the strength to choose between the two.

John Cheever

The moral flabbiness born of the exclusive worship of
the bitch-goddess SUCCESS. That — with the squalid
cash interpretation put on the word success — is our
national disease.

William James

There are many paths to the top of the mountain, but the view is always the same.

Chinese proverb

The artist is a receptacle for emotions that come from all over the place: from the sky, from the earth, from a scrap of paper, from a passing shape, from a spider's web.

Pablo Picasso

Joy is prayer – Joy is strength – Joy is love – Joy is a net of love by which you can catch souls. God loves a cheerful giver. She gives most who gives with joy. The best way to show our gratitude to God and the people is to accept everything with joy. A joyful heart is the inevitable result of a heart burning with love. Never let anything so fill you with sorrow as to make you forget the joy of the Christ risen.

Mother Teresa

He who binds to himself a joy
Does the winged life destroy;
But he who kisses the joy as it flies
Lives in Eternity's sunrise.
William Blake

There are incalculable resources in the human spirit,
once it has been set free.
Hubert H. Humphrey

Life does not cease to be funny when people die, any more than it ceases to be serious when people laugh.

George Bernard Shaw, *The Doctor's Dilemma*

Nothing can be meaner than the anxiety to live on, to live on anyhow and in any shape; a spirit with any honour is not willing to live except in its own way, and a spirit with any wisdom is not over-eager to live at all.

George Santayana

Little strokes
Fell great oaks.

Benjamin Franklin, *Poor Richard's Almanac*

We are all in the gutter,
but some of us are looking at the stars.

Oscar Wilde, *Lady Windermere's Fan*

I dimly guess what Time in Mists confounds;
Yet ever and anon a trumpet sounds
From the hid battlements of Eternity.

Francis Thompson, 'The Hound of Heaven'

Glory be to God for dappled things –
For skies of couple-colour as a brindled cow;
For rose-moles all in stipple upon trout that swim;
Fresh-firecoal chestnut-falls; finches' wings;
Landscape plotted and pieced –
fold, fallow, and plough;
And all trades, their gear and tackle and trim.

Gerard Manley Hopkins, 'Pied Beauty'

Grief can take care of itself, but to get the full value of
a joy you must have somebody to divide it with.
Mark Twain

What would the world be, once bereft
Of wet and of wildness? Let them be left,
O let them be left, wildness and wet;
Long live the weeds and the wilderness yet.
Gerard Manley Hopkins, 'Inversaid'

Oh, God, make small
The old star-blanket of the sky,
That I may fold it round me and in comfort lie.
T. E. Hulme, 'The Embankment'

Breathless, we flung us on the windy hill,
Laughed in the sun, and kissed the lovely grass.
Rupert Brooke

Awake! for Morning in the Bowl of Night
Has flung the Stone that puts the Stars to Flight:
And lo! the Hunter of the East has caught
The Sultan's Turret in a Noose of Light.

Edward Fitzgerald, 'The Rubaiyat of Omar Khayyam'

The wolf also shall dwell with the lamb, and the
leopard shall lie down with the kid; and the calf
and the young lion and the fatling together;
and a little child shall lead them.

Isaiah, XI:6

Deep peace of the Running Wave to you.
Deep peace of the Flowing Air to you.
Deep peace of the Quiet Earth to you.
Deep peace of the Shining Stars to you.
Deep peace of the Son of Peace to you.

Gaelic blessing

Our brightest blazes of gladness are commonly
kindled by unexpected sparks.

Samuel Johnson

You can't separate peace from freedom because no one
can be at peace unless he has his freedom.

Malcolm X

My heart leaps up when I behold
A rainbow in the sky:

William Wordsworth, 'My Heart Leaps Up'

Slowly, slowly, climb
Up and up Mount Fuji,
O snail.

Haiku by Kobayashi Issa

The most exciting happiness is the happiness
generated by forces beyond your control.

Ogden Nash

Happiness is the only sanction of life;
where happiness fails, existence remains a mad
and lamentable experiment.

George Santayana

What a delight it is
When, after a hundred days
Of racking my brains,
That verse that wouldn't come
Suddenly turns out well.

Tachibana Akemi, *Poems of Solitary Delights*

The comfort of having a friend may be taken away,
but not that of having had one.

Seneca

I write in the sand
The word 'great'
More than a hundred times.
Then I go back home
Dropping all thought of death.

Ishikawa Takuboku, 'I Write in the Sand'

Tell me where is fancy bred,
Or in the heart or in the head?
How begot, how nourished?

William Shakespeare, *The Merchant of Venice*

My muse is she
My love shall be.

Thomas Randolph,
'Ode to Master Anthony Stafford, to Hasten Him to the Country'

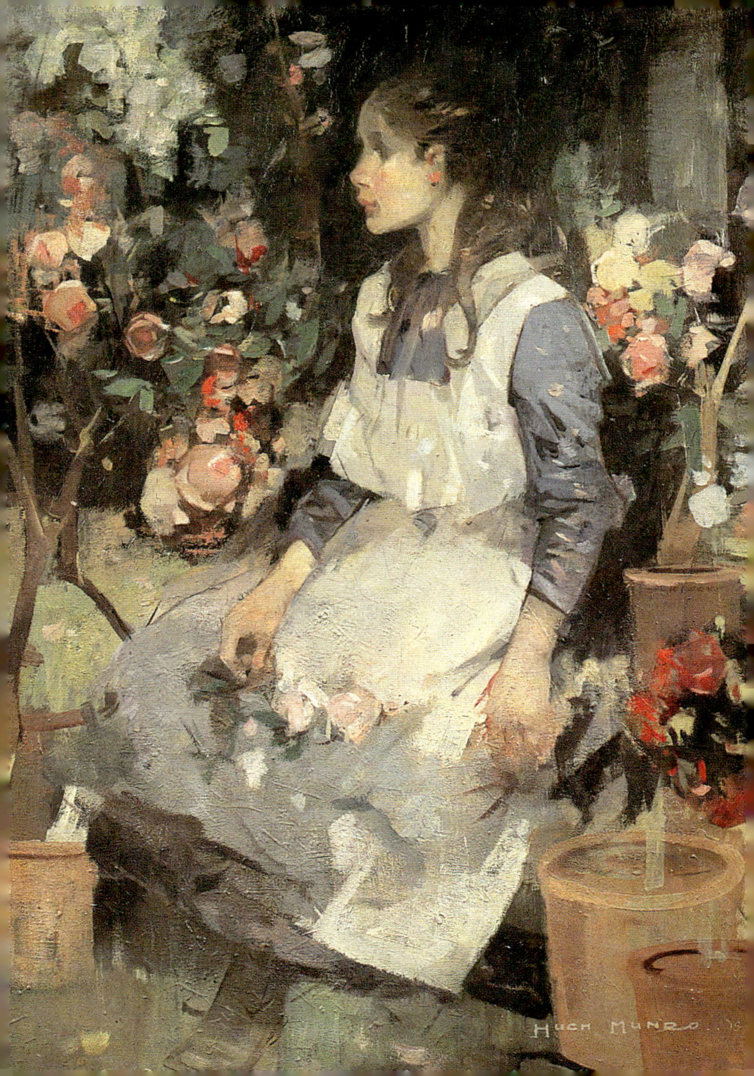
HUGH MUNRO

THE LITTLE BOOK OF INSPIRATION

I can be well content
The sweetest time of all my life
To deem in thinking spent.

Thomas, Lord Vaux, 'Of a Contented Mind'

THE LITTLE BOOK OF INSPIRATION

It nearly killed him to write this play. After his day's stint he would be physically and mentally exhausted.

Carlotta Monterey on Eugene O'Neill writing

Long Day's Journey into Night

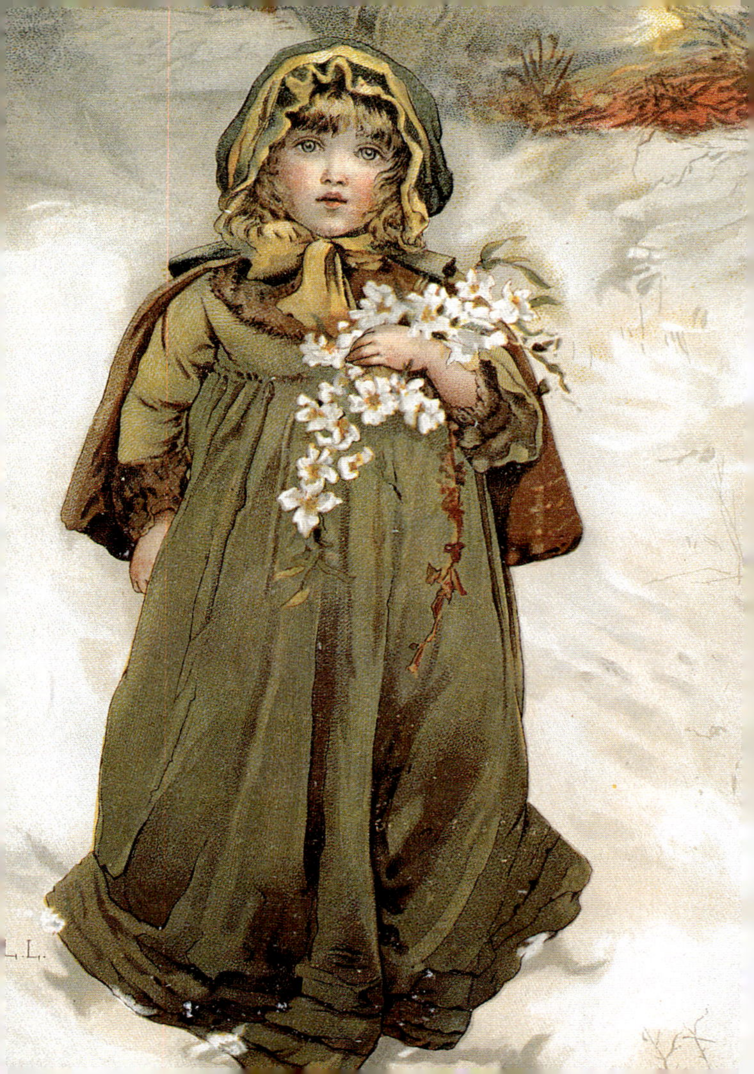

Come Holy Ghost, our souls inspire,
And lighten with celestial fire...
Book of Common Prayer

Extraordinary how potent cheap music is.
Noel Coward, *Private Lives*

Genius is one per cent inspiration,
ninety-nine per cent perspiration.
Thomas Edison, *Harper's Monthly*

If music be the food of love, play on.
William Shakespeare, *Twelfth Night*

The tools I need for my work are paper,
tobacco, food, and a little whisky.
William Faulkner

To inspire hopeless passion is my destiny.
William Makepeace Thackeray, *Pendennis*

THE LITTLE BOOK OF INSPIRATION

Attired
With sudden brightness, like a man inspired...

William Wordsworth, 'Character of the Happy Warrior'

We have two or three great moving experiences in our lives...it doesn't seem at the time that anyone else has been caught up and pounded and dazzled and astonished and beaten and broken and rescued and illuminated and rewarded and humbled in just that way ever before.

F. Scott Fitzgerald

I write when I'm inspired, and I see to it that
I'm inspired at nine o'clock every morning.

Peter de Vries

One has to go over that vast smouldering rubbish-heap
of experience, half-stifled by the fumes and dust,
scraping and delving until one finds
a few discarded valuables.

Evelyn Waugh, *The Essays*

What a delight it is
When, of a morning,
I get up and go out
To find in full bloom a flower
That yesterday was not there.

Tachibana Akemi, *Poems of Solitary Delights*

Prophets of Nature, we to them will speak
A lasting inspiration, sanctified
By reason, blest by faith.

William Wordsworth, 'The Prelude'

THE LITTLE BOOK OF INSPIRATION

It has all the contortions of the Sibyl
without the inspiration.

Samuel Johnson, *On Croft's Life of Dr Young*

Marry Ann; and at the end of a week
you'll find no more inspiration in her
than in a plate of muffins.

George Bernard Shaw, *Man and Superman*

My head is buried in the sands of
tomorrow, while my tail feathers are
singed by the hot sun of today.

John Barrymore

I remain one thing and one thing only,
and that is a clown. It places me on a far
higher plane than any politician.

Charlie Chaplin

THE LITTLE BOOK OF INSPIRATION

Unselfish and noble actions are the most radiant pages
in the biographies of souls.

Thames

The loud laugh that spoke the vacant mind.

Oliver Goldsmith

Have you had a kindness shown?
Pass it on;
'Twas not given for thee alone,
Pass it on;
Let it travel down the years,
Let it wipe another's tears,
'Till in Heaven the deed appears –
Pass it on.

Henry Burton

People at the top of the tree are those without qualifications to detain them at the bottom.

Peter Ustinov

Twixt optimist and pessimist
The difference is droll:
The optimist sees the doughnut;
The pessimist sees the hole.

Emily Dickinson, 'The Difference'

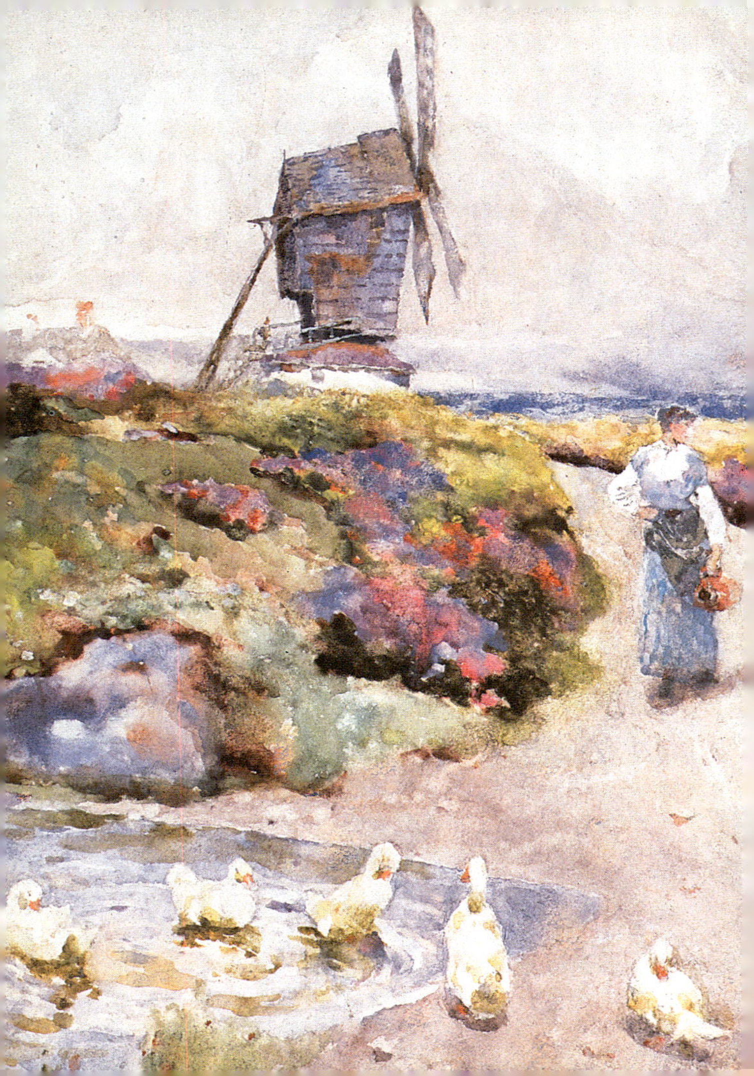

Fame is the scentless sunflower,
with gaudy crown of gold;
But friendship is the breathing rose,
with sweets in every fold.

Oliver Wendell Holmes

One must never be in haste to end a day;
there are too few of them in a lifetime.

Dale Coman

Love looks not with the eyes, but with the mind,
And therefore is wing'd Cupid painted blind.

William Shakespeare

The best mirror is an old friend.

George Herbert

To live is not to live for one's self alone;
let us help one another.

Menander

THE LITTLE BOOK OF INSPIRATION

A thing of beauty is a joy for ever:
Its loveliness increases; it will never
Pass into nothingness...

John Keats

Happy the man, and happy he alone,
He who can call today his own;
He who, secure within, can say,
Tomorrow, do thy worst, for I have lived today!

John Dryden

Be not hasty in thy spirit to be angry:
for anger resteth in the bosom of fools.

Ecclesiastes, VII:9

The sound of laughter is like the vaulted dome
of a temple of happiness.

Milan Kundera

Dare to be true;
Nothing can need a lie.
The fault that needs one most
Grows two thereby.

George Herbert

For want of a nail, the shoe was lost;
For want of a shoe, the horse was lost;
For want of a horse, the rider was lost;
For want of a rider, the battle was lost;
For want of the battle, the kingdom was lost;
And all for the want of a horseshoe nail.

Benjamin Franklin

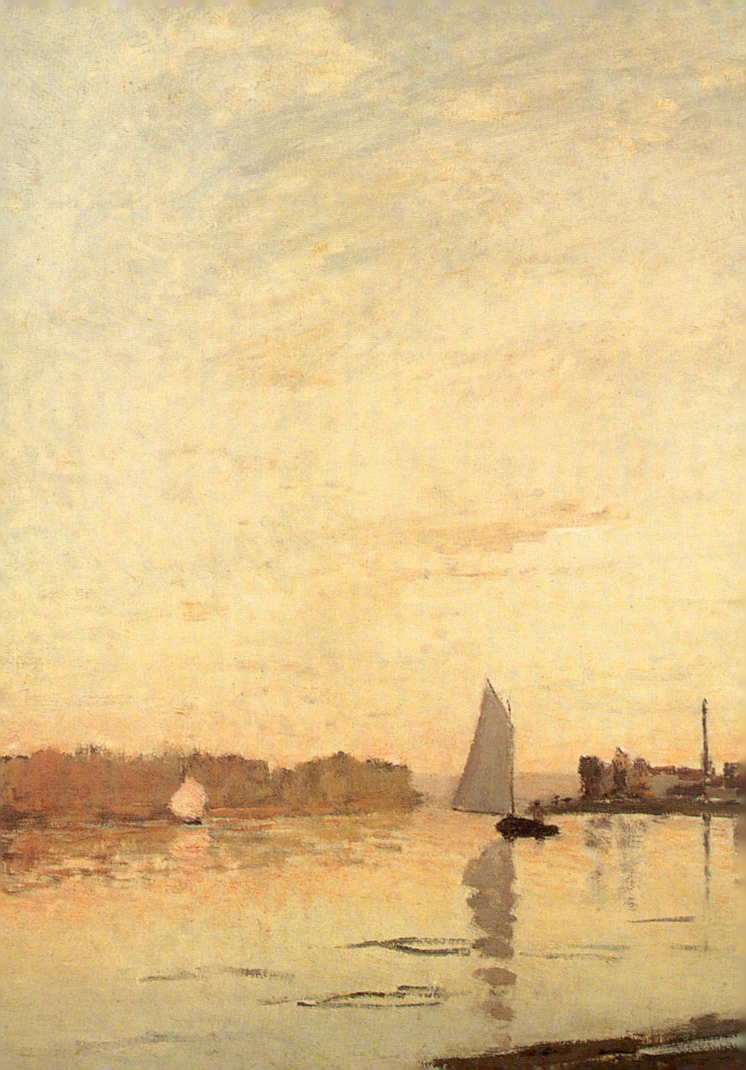

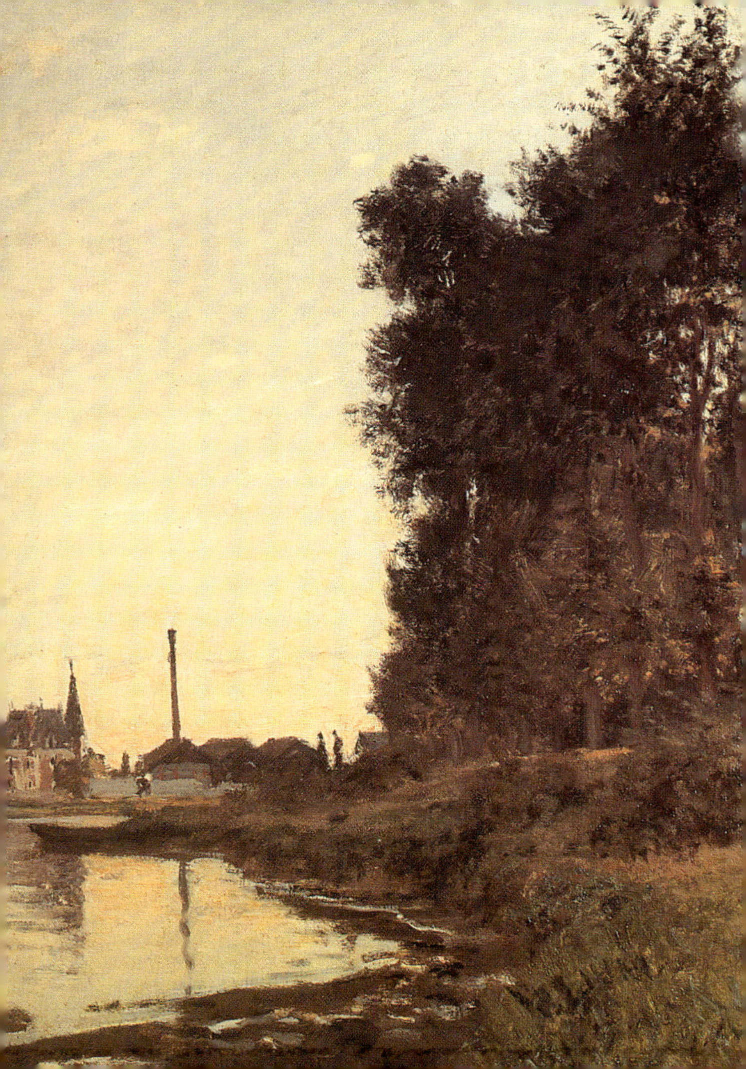

THE LITTLE BOOK OF INSPIRATION

No man can be provident of his time, who is not prudent in the choice of his company.

Jeremy Taylor

An emerald is as green as grass;
A ruby red as blood;
A sapphire shines as blue as heaven;
A flint lies in the mud.

A diamond is a brilliant stone,
To catch the world's desire;
An opal holds a fiery spark;
But a flint holds fire.

Christina Georgina Rossetti, 'Precious Stones'

What a delight it is
When, skimming through the pages
Of a book, I discover
A man written of there
Who is just like me.

Tachibana Akemi, *Poems of Solitary Delights*

THE LITTLE BOOK OF INSPIRATION

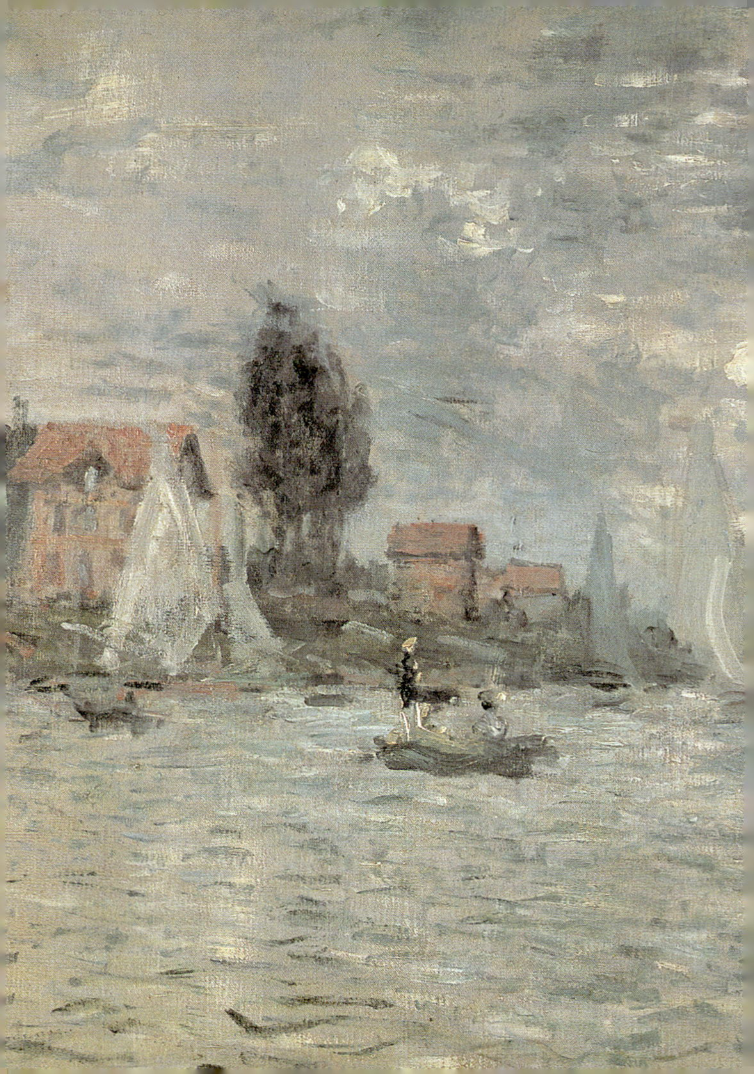

There was a definite process by which
one made friends into friends,
and it involved talking to them
and listening to them
for hours at a time.

Rebecca West

Is it so small a thing
To have enjoyed the sun,
To have lived light in the spring,
To have loved, to have thought, to have done;
To have advanced true friends,
and beat down baffling foes?

Matthew Arnold

My sole inspiration is
a telephone call from a director.

Cole Porter

NOTES ON ILLUSTRATIONS

Pages 8-9 *Impression: Sunrise, 1872* by Claude Monet (Musée Marmottan, Paris). Courtesy of The Bridgeman Art Library. **Page 11** *Mist* by N. M. Wells. Courtesy of The Foundry Creative Media Company Ltd. **Page 12** *Autumn Glow (Paddington Pond, Abinger Hammer)* by Edward Wilkins Waite (Private Collection). Courtesy of The Bridgeman Art Library. **Page 15** *Monet Painting on the Edge of a Wood, c.1887* by John Singer Sargent (Tate Gallery, London). Courtesy of The Bridgeman Art Library. **Page 16** *Valparaiso: Crepuscule in Flesh Colour and Green* by James Abbott McNeill Whistler (The Tate Gallery, London). Courtesy of The Bridgeman Art Library. **Page 19** *Cloud* by N. M. Wells. Courtesy of The Foundry Creative Media Company Ltd. **Page 21** *The Poppy Field (Les Coquelicots environs d'Argenteuil)* by Claude Monet (Musée d'Orsay, Paris). Courtesy of The Giraudon/Bridgeman Art Library. **Pages 22-3** *A Lake Scene in North Wales* by Edgar Longstaffe (Roy Miles Gallery, 29 Burton Street, London W1). Courtesy of The Bridgeman Art Library. **Page 25** *Donati's Comet over Balliol College* by William of Oxford (The Maas Gallery, London). Courtesy of The Bridgeman Art Library. **Page 27** *The Sound of Music*. Courtesy of The British Film Institute. **Page 28** *An Hour with the Poet in the Leafy Month of June* by Richard Redgrave (Christie's, London). Courtesy of The Bridgeman Art Gallery. **Page 30** *Autumn Haunts of the Kingfisher* by Edward Wilkins Waite (Private Collection). Courtesy of The Bridgeman Art Library. **Page 34** *Stoke Poges Church* by Jasper Francis Cropsey (Jonny Van Haeften Gallery, London). Courtesy of The Bridgeman Art Library. **Page 37** *Young Gardener* by Hugh Munro Spink and son Ltd., London). Courtesy of The Bridgeman Art Library. **Pages 38-9** *The Silent Highway, River Kennet, Woolhampton, Berkshire, 1911* by Edward Wilkins Waite (Private Collection). Courtesy of The Bridgeman Art Library. **Page 40** *Christmas Roses*. Courtesy of The Laurel Clark Collection. **Page 42** *Moonlight View Of Windsor Castle from the Thames* by Henry Pether (Ackermann and Johnson Ltd., London). Courtesy of The Bridgeman Art Library. **Page 45** *Waterlily Pond* by Claude Monet (National Gallery, London). Courtesy of The Bridgeman Art Library. **Page 46** *Evening Lake* by N. M. Wells. Courtesy of The Foundry Creative Media Company Ltd. **Page 48** *The Freedom of the Common, Wonham's Marsh, Surrey, 1905* by Edward Wilkins Waite (Private Collection). Courtesy of The Bridgeman Art Library. **Page 50** *The Mill on the Common, Houghton, Huntingdonshire* by David Woodlock (Bonham's, London). Courtesy of The Bridgeman Art Library. **Page 52** *The Backs, Cambridge, 1908* by Albert Goodwin (Victoria and Albert Museum). Courtesy of The Bridgeman Art Library. **Pages 54-5** *Argenteuil, Late Afternoon* by Claude Monet (Private Collection). Courtesy of The Bridgeman Art Library. **Page 57** *Into the Softness of the Stars* by N. M. Wells. Courtesy of The Foundry Creative Media Company Ltd. **Pages 58-9** *The Boats: Regatta at Argenteuil, c.1874* by Claude Monet (Musée D'Orsay, Paris). Courtesy of The Giraudon/Bridgeman Art Library.

Acknowledgements: The Publishers wish to thank everyone who gave permission to reproduce the quotes in this book. Every effort has been made to contact the copyright holders, but in the event that an oversight has occurred, the publishers would be delighted to rectify any omissions in future editions of this book. *Good News Study Bible*, published by Thomas Nelson, 1996, extracts reprinted with their kind permission; *Penguin Book of Japanese Verse*, translated by Geoffrey Bownas and Anthony Thwaite, published by Penguin 1964, and reprinted with their permission; Robert Frost reprinted from *The Poetry of Robert Frost*, by permission of Jonathan Cape and the Estate of Robert Frost, and Peter A. Gilbert, USA; Ogden Nash, from *Verses from 1929* on reprinted by permission of Curtis Brown, Ltd. Copyright © 1942 by Ogden Nash, renewed; George Bernard Shaw, reprinted courtesy of the Society of Authors on behalf of the Estate of George Bernard Shaw, Anita Brookner reprinted courtesy of Jonathan Cape, Milan Kundera translated by Heim, reprinted courtesy of Alfred A. Knopf Inc.

3